Do-it-yourself Magic

by Ruth Chew

HASTINGS HOUSE · PUBLISHERS

New York, N.Y. 10016

This edition is published in 1987 by Hastings House by arrangement
with Scholastic Book Services, a division of Scholastic Magazines, Inc.
Copyright 1987 by Ruth Chew.

Library of Congress Catalog Card Number 87-81386

ISBN 0-8038-9299-3

Hastings House, Publishers
9 E. 40th Street
New York, New York 10016

Distribution to the trade by
Kampmann & Company, Inc.
New York, New York

Printed in the United States of America

10 9 8 7 6 5 4 3 2 1

For my grandson, Jonathan Charles Silver

1

"Wow! Rachel, look at that!" Scott Walker grabbed his sister's arm and dragged her over to the shop window of the big discount store on Church Avenue.

Rachel looked at a red and green model car in the window. "That looks like those funny-looking cars we saw racing each other at the fair in the country last summer."

"It's a stock car racer," Scott said.

Rachel looked hard at the car. "There's no price." She saw a flat box with a picture of the car on it. "No wonder. It's just for display. You have to put it together yourself. Remember the trouble you had trying to build that sports car? In the end, Daddy had to do it. Even then it was lopsided."

"You could help me." Scott walked over to the door of the discount store. "Come on, Rachel. Let's see how much the model costs."

Rachel liked looking at the things in this store. It was bigger than the others on Church Avenue. Everything from school supplies to blue jeans was for sale here.

Scott walked down the aisle of toys. Rachel followed him, looking at everything on the shelves.

"Here it is, Rachel!" Scott picked up a box with a picture of the red and green car on it. "See, I was right. It says *racing stock car* on the lid. And look what else it says: *Easy to assemble!* There's a man to drive it. He's just the right size."

Rachel looked at the price tag. "That costs almost seven dollars, Scott."

Scott put down the box. The two children went over to a bin with a big sign over it:

MARKED DOWN

The things here were all either dented or dirty or missing a part. Rachel saw a big, blue box with pictures of something that could be clouds on it. In pale blue letters that seemed to drift in and out of the clouds, Rachel could just make out the words *The Build-Anything Kit*.

The box had a bashed-in corner, but there was no hole in it. Rachel picked it up.

"It's heavy." Rachel shook the box. "And it rattles. There must be a lot of parts."

"Let me see that." Scott leaned over to read the words in the clouds. "We could use this to build our own stock car racer. Look at the price, Rachel!"

"Seventy-nine cents, and don't forget the tax." Rachel took two quarters out of her pocket. "I still have this left from my last week's allowance."

Scott pulled out a quarter and two dimes. "I've got almost as much as you do. Together we have more than enough to buy the kit."

Rachel carried the blue box to the checkout counter.

The man at the counter looked at the box and then at the two children. "You understand that you can't return things that are marked down?"

"Why was this marked down?" Rachel asked.

"It was one of our high-priced sets, but it's been on the shelf for months," the man said. "I guess people thought it cost too much. We marked it down this morning because the box was damaged from so many children shaking it."

"Do you think the things inside are broken?" Scott wanted to know.

"That's a chance you'll have to take," the store man said. "I'm not allowed to open the box, but I understand there was nothing breakable in the kit."

Rachel never knew why she suddenly wanted the kit so much. "We'll take it," she said and put her two quarters on the counter.

Scott laid his money down beside hers.

2

The store man rang up the sale on his cash register and put a nickel and four pennies change on the counter.

Scott took the pennies and gave the nickel to his sister. "That makes us just about even," he said.

The store man laughed. He put the Build-Anything Kit into a plastic shopping bag with two handles. "You can take turns carrying it or you can each grab a handle. I hope it does everything you want it to."

"Thank you." Rachel took the plastic bag and carried it out of the store. It was lucky that her schoolbooks were in a backpack so she could use both hands.

The kit seemed to get heavier with every step she took.

At the first cross street, Rachel said, "Maybe we should each take a handle."

Scott carried his books on his back, too. "Hand me that bag, Rachel. I'll take it the rest of the way home."

Rachel was older than Scott. She didn't think he was stronger than she was, but she wasn't going to argue now. She gave him the plastic bag, making sure he had a good grip on it.

Scott lifted the bag and held it from the bottom.

The two children made their way along the crowded sidewalk. They passed a hardware store, a little dress shop, a dancing school, and a flower store with enormous stuffed toys in the window.

When they came to the fruit stand, Scott put the plastic bag down on the pavement. Rachel grabbed one of the han-

dles. "We've tried taking turns," she said. "Now let's carry it together."

Scott took hold of the other handle. Both children were surprised at how easy it was to carry the plastic bag now. They turned the corner onto the street where they lived.

Their house was halfway down the block. They could see their mother waiting on the front stoop. She was looking up and down the street.

Mrs. Walker didn't wait for Scott and Rachel to reach the house. She ran down the street to meet them. "It's half past three on Friday!" she said. "Don't tell me *both* of you were kept after school for talking in class!" She bent over to give them each a kiss.

"We went into the discount store, Mom," Scott told her. "Wait till we show you the bargain we got!"

"I'll *have* to wait to see it," Mrs. Walker

said. "Your dad telephoned and asked me to meet him after work. He wants to take me out for supper. Would you mind having TV dinners tonight?"

"Fried chicken?" Scott asked.

"Yes." Mrs. Walker smiled. "I know that's your favorite."

The three of them walked down the street to the old limestone house and climbed the front stoop. Mrs. Walker unlocked the door, and they went in.

"You'd better hurry and get your after-school snack," Mrs. Walker said, "or you won't be hungry at dinnertime." She started up the stairs. "I'll have to rush and change my clothes to go out."

Scott and Rachel left their backpacks and the plastic bag in the front hall and headed for the kitchen.

3

When their mother came back down-stairs, Scott and Rachel were busy smearing butter and blackberry jam on English muffins.

"You'll need something to wash those down." Mrs. Walker took a container of milk out of the refrigerator and filled two glasses. Then she spun around as if she were dancing. "How do you like my new dress?"

"Nice," Rachel said.

Scott looked at the dress. "I saw one just like it last week in a shop window on

Church Avenue. I wanted to buy it for your birthday, Mom."

His mother laughed. "Draw me a picture instead." She looked at the kitchen clock. "I'd better leave now," she said. "I don't want to keep your Dad waiting. Be sure to change out of your school clothes.

Meantime, try not to get any jam on them. Oh, I almost forgot to tell you I'm expecting a package. Rachel, would you please sign for it?" Mrs. Walker went to get her coat and hat.

"Have a good time, Mother," Rachel called.

Rachel and Scott heard the front door bang as their mother went out. They finished their after-school snack and put the dirty dishes into the dishwasher. Then they went to get their books from the front hall.

Rachel always liked to do her homework right away on Friday afternoon so she'd have the rest of the weekend free. She carried her backpack upstairs to her room.

Scott put his backpack on so he could carry the plastic bag with the Build-Anything Kit up to his room at the back of the house.

Rachel changed into a T-shirt, jeans,

and sneakers. She sat down at her desk to do her homework.

Rachel read her social studies book and answered some questions. She was just going to start her math when Scott came into the room. "Look what I built."

"Is that a garbage truck or a tricycle?" Rachel asked.

"It's a stock car racer," Scott told her. "There aren't any directions, and I couldn't find four wheels the same size."

"I guess that's why the kit was marked down," Rachel said. "We should never have bought it."

"You were the one who told the man we'd take it," Scott reminded her.

Rachel knew he was right. "I'd better look at the kit, Scott. Bring along your racer, and we'll see if we can make it better." She got up from her desk and went down the hall to her brother's room.

Scott had left the big blue box open on

the floor. Rachel got down on her hands and knees to look at the different things in the box. There were a great many, and they were all jumbled together.

"The first thing we have to do is sort this stuff." Rachel began to take out the things one at a time. She laid them side by side in the lid of the box. She picked up what looked like a little steering wheel. Rachel bent over to get a good look at it and found she had picked up something else as well. "Scott, take a look at this."

"I never saw anything like that in the box." Scott stared at the clear plastic tool. It looked like a hammer with two heads. One hammerhead was much smaller than the other.

"I didn't see it, either, till I picked it up." Rachel put the double hammer in the lid of the Build-Anything Kit. Then she reached into the blue box for an axle.

"Rachel," Scott whispered. "Look!" He pointed to the lid.

The little plastic hammer had disappeared!

4

"The hammer's gone!" Scott said.

"I put it right on top of all that junk," Rachel told him. "Maybe it slid down inside. Clear plastic is hard to see. You never even noticed the hammer when you were making your whatever-it-is." She reached into the lid and picked up the first thing she touched.

Scott grabbed her wrist. "Now it's back again!"

Rachel saw that she had the double hammer in her hand. She thought for a minute. "I guess it's hard to see when it's mixed with all those things. They're all different colors. What do you have that's plain and flat?"

Scott went over to his desk. "Here's the

math test the teacher returned today. I only used one side of the paper."

Rachel took the hammer over to the desk. Scott put the math paper blank-side–up on top of his math book. Rachel laid the hammer on the paper. At once the hammer vanished.

Scott sat on his heels to look at the paper sideways. "There's no sign of it." He reached over to the place on the paper where he thought the hammer would be. "I can feel it, and I can see it now, too!"

Rachel felt a little thrill of excitement as she watched the hammer come into view the second Scott touched it. As soon as he lifted his finger, the little plastic tool could not be seen.

Scott took a deep breath before he picked up the hammer. Rachel knew that he was trying not to show he was scared.

He stood up and turned the hammer over and over in his hands. As long as he was holding it, both children could see it. "There's some writing on the handle." Scott said. "SIZER." He thought for a minute. "Maybe that's the name of the maker."

"Well, it's part of the Build-Anything Kit," Rachel said. "Why don't we try to figure out what it's good for—besides getting lost? What did you do with that car you built?"

Scott had left his car on the floor beside the Build-Anything Kit. He took the hammer over and began to tap the wheels. When he hit a wheel with the big hammer, the wheel became smaller. Scott tried tapping with the little hammer. At once the wheel became bigger.

"Look at that!" Scott said.

"Now we know what the word SIZER means," Rachel said. "This hammer changes the size of things."

Scott sat down on the floor and set to

work to match up the wheels of his racer.

Rachel got down on her hands and knees and leaned over the big blue box. She pulled out all the things that might be part of a car and placed them on the floor.

Scott fished around in the pile she made. "Here's a windshield!"

The windshield was too small for the car Scott was building. He tapped it with the little hammer. Then it was too big. He had to work very slowly with both hammerheads until it was just the right size. "I'm beginning to get the hang of this thing," he told Rachel. "It works much too fast if you're not careful."

Rachel didn't know as much about cars as Scott did, but she wanted the racer to look like the ones at the country fair. She went to get her crayons, some paper, and a pair of scissors.

Rachel drew wiggly green stripes and circles on the paper. She cut them out. "Let me have the sizer for a minute, Scott. I want to see if it will work on something that isn't part of the kit."

5

"I've almost finished putting the car to-gether," Scott said. "You can have the sizer in a minute."

Rachel looked at the little red car. "It's much better than it was, Scott, but it still doesn't look like a stock car racer."

Scott scratched his head. Then he grinned. "It's the tires. Those racers all had tires much bigger than regular cars do." Scott tapped away with the small hammer until the tires were just the size he wanted. "How's that?"

"Better," Rachel said.

Scott handed Rachel the sizer. She gently tapped the wiggly green stripe she had made.

"It's getting bigger," Scott said. "I thought maybe the Build-Anything Kit was like a computer and was programmed by the sizer. But if the sizer works on things that aren't in the kit, it *can't* be a computer."

"No," Rachel agreed. Then she said in a whisper, "But all along I've had the feeling it was *magic*."

Neither of the children said anything for a little while.

Rachel started to check the size of the green stripe against the racing car.

"It's a little too big now," Scott said.

Rachel made the stripe smaller. "Do you have any glue, Scott?"

Scott went to get a jar of rubber cement from his desk top.

Rachel glued on the wiggly racing

stripe. Scott helped her decide where to put the circles.

"It looks even better than the seven-dollar model in the discount store," Rachel said. "It looks just like the stock car racers we saw at the fair."

Scott lay down on his stomach to admire his work. "This is the best thing I ever built. There's only one thing the car in the store had that this one doesn't."

"What's that?" Rachel wanted to know.

"A driver," Scott said.

Rachel was still holding the sizer. She didn't know what made her tap Scott with it, but before she knew what was happening, he was only three inches high.

Rachel was so surprised that she couldn't speak. She just stared at her brother.

Scott looked around and caught sight of his sister's sneakers. He craned his neck to look up at her face. "How did you get that big?" His voice was so tiny that Rachel could hardly hear him.

"I'm not big, Scott," she said. "You're small."

Scott put his hands over his ears. "Well, try not to shout." He took a good look at the car he had built. "This is great! I'm just the right size for it now!"

Rachel was sure she could never have done this if she had tried.

Scott opened the car door and climbed in. "Rachel, there's a key in the dash-board!"

A second later Rachel heard the purr of a little motor. Scott drove his car across the floor. He steered it around the desk and drove under the chair. Then he went in and out of the open closet and all around the bed.

Rachel pushed the magic sizer deep into the pocket of her jeans for safekeeping. If she put it down, she wouldn't be able to see it. Then how could she get Scott back to his usual size? It was a scary thought.

Scott zoomed past her ankle in the little car. He leaned out of the window to shout, "Thank you, Rachel. This is fun!"

The front doorbell rang twice, loud and long. Whoever was there must be in a hurry.

Rachel ran downstairs.

6

Rachel peeked through the venetian blind on the front door.

The Parcel Service man was standing on the stoop outside. He had a package in his hand.

Rachel opened the door. "My mother told me she was expecting something," she said. "She asked me to sign for it."

Just then Rachel heard a bumping noise. It seemed to be coming from the stairs in the hall right behind her.

"Sign here." The Parcel Service man held out his clipboard and handed Rachel a pen.

She wrote her name on the line marked with an X. Then the man gave her the package. He turned to go back to his truck.

Before Rachel could close the door, something shot past her onto the stoop outside.

It was the little stock car racer!

Bump! Bump! Bump! The racer went rolling down the front steps of the house.

The Parcel Service man jumped out of the way. "That thing nearly knocked me over. You'd better take it back inside."

Rachel dropped the package on the chair by the door. She took the magic sizer out of her pocket and rushed out onto the front stoop.

She looked for the little car on the sidewalk in front of the house, but it wasn't there.

Then she saw it. The stock car racer had rolled into the street. It was right in

front of the Parcel Service truck. And the truck was starting to move!

Rachel was frantic. She didn't have time to think. She was never sure if she ran down the steps or the magic sizer pulled her down. Rachel had never moved so fast in her life.

The sizer seemed to be flying ahead of

her. Rachel held on to it and dived toward
the little racing car.

Crash!

The magic sizer smashed down onto
the racer. Rachel didn't know which hammerhead hit the car.

Screech!

The Parcel Service truck skidded to a

stop to keep from slamming into a big red and green car.

For a minute the Parcel Service man just stared. Then he drove away slowly down the street.

Rachel stared at the car, too, and then at the sizer in her hand. She must have hit the stock car racer with the small hammer. The car was much bigger now.

Rachel looked inside the car.

Scott was sitting behind the steering wheel. He turned his head and saw her. "Rachel, now *you're* small! Did you hit yourself on the head?"

"Don't be silly, Scott," Rachel said. "Look around. I'm not any smaller than usual. You're back to your regular size. Don't you know you were almost run over by the Parcel Service truck? How could you be stupid enough to drive that toy car into the street?"

"I didn't do it on purpose," Scott told her.

"Why did you do it?" Rachel asked.

"I heard the most terrible rasping noise, and then you rushed out of my room," Scott said.

Rachel thought for a second. "That was the doorbell. The Parcel Service man was leaning on it."

"How was I to know? I thought it was some kind of siren, and I tried to follow you. Next thing I knew the car was rolling down the stairs. I was afraid it would turn over if I tried to stop." Scott grinned. "That car did tricks just like the stock car racers at the fair. It went down the stairs and rolled out the front door and down the stoop. And it stayed right-side–up the whole time!"

7

Rachel wanted to see what the racer was like inside. She looked through the window.

Scott opened the door. "Get in, Rachel."

She climbed into the car and shut the door.

"I didn't know you knew how to drive," Rachel said.

"This car drives like the 'Dodge 'em' cars at Coney Island. I'll show you."

Scott stepped on the button on the floor. The big stock car jumped forward and roared down the block to the corner. Scott took his foot off the button. He steered the car around the corner onto Albemarle Road. It coasted to a stop halfway down the block.

"Isn't this fun?" Scott said.

"Doesn't this car have brakes?" Rachel asked him.

Scott looked at the floor of the car. "I forgot to put them in when I was building it. But then I never put in the key that turns the motor on, or the button that makes the car go."

Rachel looked at the double hammer she had in her hand. "Scott, the sizer seems to do what it wants to, not only what we want it to."

Scott grinned. "I was wondering how you got me back to my right size so fast. Suppose you made me twice as big?"

"It's not funny, Scott," Rachel said. "Maybe we shouldn't use the sizer on ourselves."

A woman came out of the house in the middle of the block. She tapped on the car window. Rachel rolled down the window.

The woman looked hard at Scott and Rachel. "I know you children live in the neighborhood, but I've never seen this crazy-looking car around here before. Where is the driver?"

Scott was sitting behind the steering wheel. All of a sudden both children remembered that neither of them was old enough to drive a car.

Scott didn't know what to say.

The woman frowned. "You'd better go and get your father to move that car. It's blocking my driveway." She walked back to the sidewalk and stood there, watching.

Rachel opened the car door. "I'll make sure that the car is moved," she said to the woman. "It might take a few minutes. You could get your car started in the meantime." Rachel began to walk down the sidewalk.

The woman went into her house.

Scott stepped on the button. The stock car racer started down the street. Rachel ran to keep up with it.

Scott took his foot off the button. The car went slower and slower. It stopped just before it came to the corner.

Rachel stood on the sidewalk. "What luck! Here's a parking space! Just back into it, Scott."

"I can't," Scott told her. "The car only goes forward."

Rachel remembered how hard it was to control the "Dodge 'em" cars in Coney Island. The next street was Ocean Parkway. It was always crowded with traffic. She didn't dare let her brother drive around the corner.

Rachel turned around to see if there was anyone else on the street. "Scott, look!"

The woman who had been talking to them was not taking her car out after all. Instead she was standing in the street, talking to two policemen in a patrol car. And she was pointing to the stock car racer with Scott behind the steering wheel!

8

"Scott," Rachel said, "get out of the car and stand clear of it. Hurry!"

Scott did as he was told.

Rachel was still holding the magic sizer.

Wham! She hit the stock car racer as hard as she could with the big hammer.

"Oops! I must have hit it too hard." Rachel bent down and picked up a tiny car. It was no bigger than a Matchbox toy. She handed it to her brother. "We can try to make it the right size later."

"It's okay the way it is," Scott said.

"We'd better go home. I left the front door open." Rachel raced back the way they had come.

Scott ran after her.

They had to pass the woman who was talking to the two policemen. She rushed over and grabbed Rachel by the arm. "Wait a minute!"

Rachel stopped running.

Scott ran to stand beside her.

The policemen were still sitting in their car. The woman called to them. "These are the children I telephoned the precinct about."

One of the policemen got out of the patrol car. He walked over to the children. "What's this I hear about you driving a big red car with green stripes?"

"You mean this?" Scott held out the tiny stock car racer.

The policeman took it from him. "Hey, Frankie, take a look! It's a perfect little

stock car. Boy, wouldn't my kid love this!
Where did you get it, sonny?"

"We made it from a kit we bought at
the discount store on Church Avenue,"
Scott told him.

The woman interrupted. "I'm not talking about that toy. This boy was driving a big, dangerous car. He must have left it around the corner on Ocean Parkway."

"Frankie, take a run around the block and see if you can spot the car. I'll stay here with the kids." He turned to the woman. "Did the car you're talking about look anything like this?" He showed her the little racer.

The woman stared. "Exactly!"

"That car should be easy to spot." The policeman at the wheel drove the patrol car around the block. In almost no time he was back.

"Sorry, lady. No sign of it," he said to the woman. "Get in the car, Bill! I just had a call about a drug pusher on East Third Street."

Bill handed Scott the little stock car racer and jumped into the patrol car. It streaked away with the siren blaring.

Scott put the toy car into his pocket. The woman turned around and went back into her house.

Scott and Rachel remembered their front door. They started running again.

9

When Rachel and Scott reached their house, the door was wide open. A man in a leather jacket was standing on the walk looking up at it. He started up the steps.

The two children dashed past the man on the front steps and ran into the house. Rachel slammed the door tight behind them.

"That man looked as if he was going to walk right in here," Scott said.

"Sh-sh!" Rachel put her finger to her lips. "I thought I heard a noise. Maybe somebody is already in the house!"

She looked through the venetian blind on the front door. The man in the leather jacket was standing near the sycamore tree in front of the house. He seemed to be waiting for someone.

Rachel's heart began to pound. She tiptoed up the stairs in the hall. Scott came after her.

The door of the big bedroom at the front of the house was open.

Rachel and Scott saw a man with red hair standing in front of the color television set on their father's dresser. The man was dressed in blue jeans and a blue denim jacket, and he had a screwdriver in his hand. He leaned over the set.

Rachel was so angry she forgot to be scared. "Get away from Daddy's television set!" She was still holding the magic sizer in her hand. Before the man could turn around to see who was screaming at him, Rachel pounded him on the back with the

large hammer. He tried to push her away, but he was already much too small.

Scott ran to the bathroom to get his toothbrush glass. When he came back, the man had shrunk to the size of a cockroach.

"Rachel, stop!" Scott cried.

Rachel put the magic sizer into the pocket of her jeans. Scott picked up the tiny man and put him into the glass.

For a while, the man just stood and looked around. Then he tried to climb up the sides of the glass, but they were too slippery. He beat on the glass with his fists and tried to kick a hole in it. It was no use.

The man was trapped. He was so small and looked so helpless that Scott began to feel sorry for him. He picked up the glass and held it in front of his face. "Don't be afraid. We won't hurt you."

The man looked through the glass at

Scott. His face was so tiny that Scott could barely see his mouth, but it seemed to be moving.

"He's talking," Scott said, "but I can't make out what he's trying to say. Let's take him downstairs to the kitchen, Rachel. The light is brighter there."

10

On their way to the kitchen Scott and Rachel had to pass the front door. Rachel peeked through the venetian blind. The man in the leather jacket had gone.

Scott carried the toothbrush glass with the little man in it to the kitchen. He set the glass on the table and sat on a chair facing it.

Rachel came into the room.

"I still can't make out what he's trying to say," Scott told her.

Rachel tore a corner off the memo pad on the shelf above the sink. She used the Eversharp pencil beside the memo pad to say in very small letters on the bit of paper

PLEASE WRITE

Rachel held the piece of paper in front of the toothbrush glass so the man could see it. He had to turn his head from one side to the other to read what she had written. Then he leaned back to look up through the open end of the glass at Rachel.

She pointed to her writing.

The man nodded.

Rachel tore another corner from the memo pad and dropped it into the toothbrush glass. The paper fell on top of the little man. He grabbed it and stepped on it to hold it down.

Rachel went to get a piece of thread from her mother's sewing cabinet. She broke off a bit of lead from the Eversharp pencil and tied it to the thread. Slowly she let the lead down into the glass until the

man could take hold of it. It was like a
thick stick in his hands.

The man got down on his hands and
knees and began to write. The paper was
bigger than he was. He made each letter
as large as he could. It took a long time.

Scott watched him. "Why don't you heat the TV dinners, Rachel? I'm hungry. I'll tell you when he's finished writing. Meantime I'll write to him." Scott picked up the Eversharp pencil.

Rachel took the TV dinners out of the freezer and read the directions. When the dinners were in the oven, she set the kitchen timer for thirty minutes and went to see how the letter writing was coming along.

"My hand is cramped from writing so small," Scott said.

The man in the toothbrush glass was making a question mark as long as his arm. He stood up and tapped on the side of the glass. Rachel bent over to see what he had written. His letter said

WHAT HAPPENED?

Rachel wrote her answer on the back of the little piece of paper she had used before.

MAGIC

She held the paper near the glass so the man could read it. "Scott, where's your letter?"

Scott's message was on a smudged scrap of paper. He had written

WHO ARE YOU?

The man read this. Then he turned over the paper in the glass and wrote

CHESTER

This took a long time.

"His name is Chester," Scott told Rachel. I guess he didn't have room on his paper to write his last name. Maybe it's a long one, like O'Hoolihan. He looks kind of like a kid in my class with that name."

Ding! That was the timer.

"We'll have to try to find out more about him later. He can't make any trouble now that he's so small." Rachel went to take the TV dinners out of the oven. She put them on the table.

Chester was sitting cross-legged in the glass. Rachel didn't know if he was hungry, but it would take so long for him to tell her that the food would get cold.

She rinsed the cap from a soda bottle. Then she used her mother's kitchen scissors to cut a little cube of chicken from her dinner. Beside it she put a kernel of corn and a very small dab of mashed potato. She wiped the scissors clean and cut another cube. This one was from her brownie. There was room for it in the bottle cap, too.

Rachel put the bottle cap on the table. She cut the corner from her paper napkin and folded it neatly. "Take Chester out of that toothbrush glass, Scott," she said. "He'll eat at the table with us."

11

Chester seemed to enjoy his dinner. He was still eating when both Scott and Rachel had finished. At last he stopped and put both hands on his stomach to show that he was full. There was still some chicken and potato left in the bottle cap, but Rachel saw that the piece of brownie was all gone.

Rachel dumped the foil trays from the TV dinners into the kitchen garbage can. "You can clean up the rest of this mess," she told her brother.

Rachel went upstairs. She wanted to see what else was in the Build-Anything Kit.

Scott put the dirty glasses and silverware into the dishwasher. He stuck his toothbrush glass in as well. Chester sat on the edge of the kitchen table and swung his legs while he watched everything that was going on.

Scott thought it would be fun to play with him. He took the stock car racer out of his pocket and put it on the table. Chester stopped swinging his legs. He stood up and walked over to the car. It was just the right size for him. Chester opened the car door and slid behind the wheel.

"This is no place for you to drive." Scott picked up the car and took it upstairs. The light was on in his room. Scott stepped inside and closed the door behind him.

Rachel was leaning over the Build-Anything Kit.

Scott held out the stock car racer so that Rachel could see Chester at the wheel. Then he put the car on the floor.

Seconds later Chester started the motor. The car leaped forward and rolled under the bed.

"I hope Chester has fun with it," Scott said. "I've had enough of driving that car."

The Build-Anything Kit was still on the floor of Scott's room. Rachel looked into the big blue box. "That's funny. You used a lot of parts to make the stock car racer, but the box is still full." She held up a rough gray block. "This looks like a stone. It feels like one, too."

Scott came over to see what she was talking about. "I don't remember anything like that in the kit."

"There are lots of them." Rachel began to build a wall of gray stones.

"Wait a minute, Rachel." Scott took a book off his desk and opened it to a picture that went across two pages. "Do you think we could build something like this?"

Rachel saw a bright-colored picture of a castle. "Let's try," she said.

The children started to build a square tower.

The stock car racer shot out from under the bed. Chester steered it around the room. The car was so small now that it could dart under the radiator and circle around each leg of Scott's desk chair.

Rachel and Scott finished their tower. They had left spaces between the blocks at the top to make notches.

Chester parked the stock car racer beside the Build-Anything Kit. He watched the children make a wall around the castle.

The top of the wall was notched, too. On each corner there was a tower.

Chester saw Rachel make an opening in one side of the wall.

"This will be the gate," she said.

Scott looked at it. "Now it's almost like a real castle."

There was a little click. Scott and Rachel turned to see the door of the stock car open. Chester stepped out. He walked quickly to the wall they had built and slipped through the open gate into the castle.

12

Rachel lay on her stomach and looked into the castle. "I don't see Chester anywhere. He must be hiding from us."

"If Chester is running around loose, he might get stepped on," Scott said. "You never should have told me to take him out of my toothbrush glass. He was safe in there. I don't want anything to happen to him, Rachel."

"Neither do I," Rachel said. "I never meant to make him quite so small. It would be my fault if something terrible happened to him." She dug far down in her jeans pocket and pulled out the magic sizer.

"What are you going to do?" Scott asked her.

"I'm going to make this gateway big enough for us to go in and get Chester." Rachel tapped the castle wall next to the gate with the little hammer.

A moment later, Scott whispered, "What's happening to the castle?"

Rachel stared. "It's getting bigger, *much* bigger."

The castle wall reached far above them. It was made of huge blocks of stone. They couldn't see Scott's bedroom now.

Rachel put the hammer back into her pocket.

Scott looked around. "There's a moat!"

The moat was crossed by a draw-bridge. On the other side of the bridge, there was another wall with a walk along the top that led from one great tower to the next. Beyond the wall Rachel could see green fields and woods that stretched away into the distance.

Two men with heavy loads of wood on their backs plodded across the bridge and through the open gate. A woman came out with a basket of laundry on her head. A little girl ran after her.

Then a group of men on horseback came riding along a winding road out of the woods. They clattered across the drawbridge and into the castle.

Rachel thought she heard music from somewhere inside the gate. It sounded like something she'd heard before, but she wasn't sure. "Come on, Scott," she said. "Let's go in."

The stone wall was so thick that it was almost like a tunnel. Rachel and Scott stepped out into a big open courtyard. They blinked in the sunlight.

"It feels like summer here, and it's still daylight," Scott said. "We had the lights turned on at home."

Rachel wrinkled her nose. "This place smells like the bridle path in Prospect Park."

"Of course. That's a stable." Scott pointed to it.

Clang! Clang! Clang!

They peeked through a doorway. A blacksmith was hammering on an anvil over a glowing fire.

Next door a man was training hawks to hunt.

Rachel kept thinking she could hear music, but there was so much going on in the courtyard that she couldn't tell where it was coming from. Everywhere there seemed to be grunting pigs, clucking hens, and screaming children.

A number of people were baking their own bread at the same time in a big stone oven. Nearby in the cookhouse Scott and Rachel saw an enormous fire. A boy was cranking a huge spit with a whole pig on it. Two men were dropping carrots and turnips and chunks of meat into a big iron pot. Rachel thought they must be making enough stew for an army.

Scott and Rachel came to a well where a woman was filling a clay jug with water. She smiled at them. "You are not from this part of the world," she said. "Your clothes are like those of the minstrel over there. Did you come with him?"

Now the children saw a red-haired man in a blue denim jacket and jeans sitting on a barrel. He was surrounded by a crowd of people.

It was Chester. And he was playing "Old Man River" on a mouth organ.

13

Rachel walked over to the crowd of people who were listening to Chester play. Scott followed her.

"It's very strange music," a young woman said, "but I like it."

The man next to her nodded. "It ought to have words. Too bad the minstrel can't sing along with those pipes."

Rachel started to sing, " 'Old Man River, that Old Man River, he don't say nothing. He must know something.' "

Scott chimed in, " 'He just keeps rolling. He keeps on rolling along.' "

Chester stopped playing to stare at Scott and Rachel.

"More! More!" the people in the crowd called. They wanted Chester to play and the children to sing the song again. Soon they were all singing along.

When Chester ran out of breath, he put

the mouth organ into his pocket. Then he climbed down from the barrel and walked over to Scott and Rachel. "You must be the kids who gave me supper."

"And you must be the burglar who wanted to steal Daddy's television set," Rachel said.

Chester looked away. "Sorry about that," he mumbled. He looked so ashamed that suddenly Rachel was sorry for him. She changed the subject. "You're a whiz with that mouth organ!"

"I'm not anything special. I just love to play," Chester told her. "I don't think these people have ever seen a mouth organ before." He looked around at the castle courtyard. "Is this more magic?"

"Yes," Rachel told him, "but we didn't mean it to be like this."

"This magic is not bad at all," Chester said. "Neither was the other—once I got used to it. At first it was scary."

Chester had freckles and a nice smile.

Rachel couldn't help liking him. She decided to wait until later to find out why he had become a burglar.

"What's your name?" he asked. "I heard you talking before, but your voices were so loud I never could make out the words."

"I'm Rachel. This is my brother, Scott."

"Thanks for letting me drive the stock car racer, Scott," Chester said. "I always wanted to drive one when I had a job with a carnival, but the racing drivers wouldn't let anybody touch their cars."

"It doesn't drive like most cars," Scott said.

"The controls are like any other car, only better," Chester told him. "The big difference is all those fancy gadgets to tell you exactly how hot the oil and the water are."

Scott thought about this. He looked at Rachel. Both of them were wondering why the racer was different for Chester than it was for them. Rachel thought she knew the answer.

"Why did you leave the car and go into the castle?" Scott asked.

"I wanted to see what the inside of the castle was like." Chester took the mouth organ out of his pocket. He started to play.

"The car wouldn't have been any fun for Chester if it wasn't a real racer," Rachel told her brother.

Scott nodded. "And a real racer

wouldn't have been safe for us."

Chester was playing "In the Good Old Summertime."

"He seems to know all the songs Daddy sings in the shower," Rachel whispered. She and Scott joined in with the words. The crowd gathered around them again.

Before long everybody was singing. They thought the words of this song were very funny. One young man called the girl next to him "Tootsie-wootsie." This made them both laugh so hard they couldn't sing.

Suddenly everybody was quiet except for Chester and Rachel and Scott.

Rachel saw a tall man walking toward them. He was dressed in a long blue tunic and carried a pole with a brass ball on top. The people bowed and made way for him.

Chester put away his mouth organ. Scott and Rachel stopped singing.

The tall man walked over to them. "As the steward here, I wish to welcome the minstrels and ask if they will dine tonight in the great hall and entertain the lord of the castle."

Scott bowed. Chester looked at him and bowed, too. Rachel remembered a movie she had seen on television last week. She made the best dancing school curtsy she could manage in jeans.

"Thank you, sir," she said. "We are honored by your invitation."

14

After the steward left, Chester took out his mouth organ and played "Old MacDonald Had a Farm." Rachel was surprised at how much these grown-up people enjoyed the song. They barked and meowed and oinked. Finally, they took each other by the hand and began to skip back and forth in a kind of round dance.

It was not until the steward came back again that the crowd would let Chester stop playing.

The steward led Chester and the two children into a very large room with a high ceiling. There were shields along the walls and banners hanging from the rafters. A long table ran down one side of the room, and the stone floor was covered with rushes.

"This is the great hall of the castle," the steward whispered. "And before you is the earl, his countess, and Lady Isabel."

Rachel saw a man in a beautiful embroidered tunic. Beside him was a lady and a girl not much older than Rachel. The rest of the people at the table were men. All of them were dressed in clothes that were much nicer than the people in the courtyard wore.

The table was piled high with food. More food was being brought in by boys carrying trays. Some of them were younger than Rachel and others were teenagers. They, too, were all well dressed.

On the other side of the hall there was another, smaller table. When the boys had served all the people at the big table, they put the trays down on the small table and sat down to eat. The steward showed Chester, Scott, and Rachel where they could sit on a long bench here. One of the boys put a wooden platter in front of Chester and another in front of the two children. He loaded the platters with stew from a tray on the table.

"We need another plate," Scott told him.

The boy pointed to the other people in the room. Each pair of diners was sharing a platter. "It's the custom here," the boy explained. "The minstrel makes an uneven number, so he has a platter to himself."

There were no forks. The men and boys cut up the meat with knives that they wore on their belts. Chester had a pocket-knife that he used. He cut up the meat for Rachel and Scott. They ate with their fingers.

"I didn't have a fork at your house, either," Chester reminded them.

"We didn't have the right-size fork for you," Rachel told him. "We weren't expecting you to come to our house. Why did you?"

Chester didn't answer.

Scott saw that Chester's face had turned bright pink. "This is the second dinner we've had today," Scott said.

Rachel licked her fingers. "Now I know why those men were putting so much stuff in that pot. It's so good I wish I had a second helping."

"No sooner said than done." The boy

who had served them smiled. He filled the wooden platter again. "Everybody here is well fed."

"But why are you here?" Scott asked. "You don't look like a servant."

"Of course I'm not a servant!" the boy said. "My father is a knight, and someday I'll be a knight, too. But I can't be knighted unless I'm trained to be one. I'm a page here. When I'm older, I'll be a squire and serve one of the knights."

Rachel looked at the big table. "Are all those men knights?"

The boy shook his head. "Can't you see that one of them is a friar?"

Rachel felt foolish. She hadn't noticed the man in the brown habit of a monk. "Why is he here?" she asked.

"You don't know anything, do you?" The boy laughed. "Somebody in the castle has to be able to read!"

15

When the meal was finished, the steward walked over to Chester and the children. "Come with me."

He led them to the table where the knights were sitting. They stopped right in front of the earl.

"Here are the minstrels you heard in the courtyard, my lord." The steward bowed and left.

"I bid you welcome to my house," the

earl said. "And I would like to hear your songs."

"Thank you, my lord." Chester made a deep bow. He took the mouth organ out of his pocket and began to play.

He played all the songs the crowd in the courtyard liked so much. The earl and his knights seemed to enjoy them, too. They laughed and clapped their hands, but they didn't sing along. Lady Isabel watched her mother and father. She didn't clap until they did.

Chester played "Yankee Doodle" and "Take Me Out to the Ball Game." Then he stopped.

"Now," the earl said, "tell us about your travels."

Chester rubbed his chin. "I've had a most unusual day, my lord. I'll try to remember it for you."

All the people at the big table stopped

talking and leaned forward to listen.

Chester began, "It was late in the day. Marty and I were walking past a row of old houses. Marty saw that the door of one of them was wide open. 'Why don't you go in and see if there's something we could use in there?' he said. 'You could just pick it up and be off.'

" 'That's a good way to get into trouble.' I told him. I started to walk past the house.

" 'Look,' Marty said. 'The door's still open. And there are no lights on in that house. I'll bet nobody's home. You could be in and out like a flash.'

" 'Forget it, Marty. Let's go get a pizza.' I grabbed his arm and tried to pull him away.

"Marty's a big guy. I couldn't get him to budge.

" 'You're a coward, Chet!' He swung

me around to face the open door. 'Now get in there and cop something or I'm finished with you for good. '

"Now, I wasn't going to let Marty call me a coward. Next thing I knew I had run up the front steps of the house and up the stairs inside as well."

Chester looked nervous now. Rachel again found herself feeling sorry for him.

The earl was waiting for the rest of the story.

Chester stood as tall as he could and swallowed a couple of times. Then he went on.

"At the top of the stairs there was a hallway with a lot of doors. I opened the first door and went inside. There was a television set in the room. That's the kind of thing you can always sell."

The earl held up his hand. "What is this set you're talking about?"

Chester stared at him. Then he looked

around at the knights and the banners. He thought for a minute. "It's a box with a glass window that can show you almost anything you want to see—dancing, singing, people fighting, playing games, wild animals, just everything."

The earl smiled. "So of course you were glad your friend forced you to do the bold deed."

"I wasn't all that glad," Chester said. "But I took out my screwdriver and was going to take the set when someone started yelling and hitting me on the back. I tried to get away, but I couldn't. Then I heard voices so loud they hurt my ears. A giant hand picked me up and dropped me into a tower of glass. I tried to climb out, but the walls were too slippery. I was caught in a trap, and I couldn't escape!"

16

No one in the great hall made a sound as Chester told his story. They all listened to every word.

He didn't stop till he came to the part where he slipped through the open gate into the castle. "I found myself in a sunny courtyard with a blue sky overhead." He took out his mouth organ and played "Oh, What a Beautiful Morning." Rachel and Scott sang the words.

The earl stood up. "A wonderful tale! I never heard anything like it. Steward, give this to the minstrel." He handed a silk purse to the steward.

Chester bowed. He took the purse and slipped it into his jacket pocket. Then he bowed again. "Thank you, my lord."

Dinner was over. Outdoors the sun had set. The room was getting dark.

The earl and his countess were first to leave the hall. Then their daughter, the Lady Isabel, followed with the friar.

Rachel smiled at the other girl. Lady Isabel gave a shy smile in return.

Next the knights and their squires went out.

Now it was up to the pages to clear the food from the tables. They took it out to the courtyard and gave it to the poor people who were waiting there in the twilight.

The pages returned to climb onto the bare tables. They folded their woolen cloaks to make pillows under their heads. Then they lay down to sleep.

The steward finished lighting a few stubby candles set in iron holders on the walls. He came over to Chester and the two children. "You are welcome to spend the night here," he said. He looked around at the sleeping pages. Then he walked out of the room, holding the pole with the brass ball on top.

"Everybody seems to go to bed early here." Chester used the bench as a step to get onto the table. He reached down to help Rachel, and then Scott, climb up.

There was plenty of room for all of them to lie down. Chester took off his

jacket and started to fold it to make a pillow.

"Oh, I almost forgot this." He took out the silk purse and opened it. "Let's see what we have here." He poured out a handful of silver coins. "These aren't like anything we have at home, but they may come in handy. It looks as if the dream will last for a while." He thought for a minute. "It doesn't seem like a dream. You said it was magic, Rachel. Can you tell me more about it?"

The candles along the wall were getting shorter. One of them flickered and went out.

Scott lay down on the table. He turned over on his stomach and rested his head on his arms. A moment later he was asleep.

Rachel spoke in a whisper so as not to disturb her brother or any of the other sleeping boys. She told Chester about the Build-Anything Kit. "There's a little gadget in the kit that makes things bigger and smaller," Rachel told him.

Chester heard how they built the stock car racer. "I had fun with that," he said.

The last candle went out. The great hall was very dark. Rachel curled up into a ball like a tired kitten. She fell asleep with Scott on one side of her and Chester on the other.

17

Rachel woke to the sound of a rooster crowing. She sat up and looked around. It was dark in the great hall of the castle, but, through one of the tall windows, Rachel saw that the sky outside was turning gray.

The page boys were sleeping soundly. So was Scott. And Chester was snoring. Rachel felt stiff all over. She wiggled over to the edge of the tabletop and stepped onto the long bench and from there to the floor.

Rachel tiptoed across the rushes on the floor to the door of the hall. She slipped out into the cool morning air.

The well was on the other side of the courtyard. Rachel went over to it. An iron spout jutted from the wall above the well, and water was dripping from it into a stone basin.

Rachel cupped her hands to take a drink. Then she washed her face and ran her damp fingers through her hair.

"Good morning," someone said.

Rachel looked up to see Lady Isabel. "Good morning," she answered.

A woman in an apron was standing behind the earl's daughter. She was holding an armful of linen, a little silver box, and a brush and comb.

Rachel smiled at her. The woman bobbed up and down in a funny little curtsy.

"Ethel is going to wash my hair," Lady Isabel said.

Rachel watched as Ethel first unbraided Lady Isabel's long hair and then wrapped her from the neck down in yards of linen. After that, Lady Isabel bent over the stone basin and let the water drip on her head.

Ethel opened the silver box and took out a cake of soap. She used this to wash Lady Isabel's hair and then carefully put the soap back into the box.

When the cold water had rinsed away all the lather, Ethel used the linen to dry Lady Isabel's hair. Finally she set to work combing it.

While Ethel was busy with the braids, Lady Isabel said, "I'm glad you came. It's so lonely here. There's no one my age I can talk to."

"What about the page boys?" Rachel asked.

"I'm not allowed to be alone with men and boys," Lady Isabel told her, "except for the friar." She lowered her voice to a whisper. "He's teaching me to *read*! Isn't that wonderful? And he's promised not to tell my mother. She thinks all a girl should know is how to sew. I hate sewing."

"So do I," Rachel said.

The sun was up now, and people were coming into the courtyard. The door of the great hall was open. Page boys were running in and out carrying trays of food.

"You'd better go back. They'll be serving breakfast soon," Lady Isabel said. "Before you go, tell me your name."

"It's Rachel. And I'm glad I met you, too." Rachel ran back to the great hall.

Scott and Chester were looking for her.

"You had us worried," Chester said. "We thought something might have happened to you."

"I didn't want to wake you," Rachel said. "I went out to get a drink of water, and I made a friend."

18

Nobody was sleeping on the tables in the great hall now. The knights were all seated in their places before the earl and his family came in. Rachel, Scott, and Chester were at the smaller table, just as they had been the night before.

The page boys set out brown bowls and filled them with steaming porridge. There were spoons made of horn for the people at the main table, but Rachel and the others had to eat with crude wooden spoons that looked like scoops. Rachel didn't mind. She was hungry.

When the bowls were cleared away, the pages put down wooden platters and brought out trays of cold meat. Rachel and Scott again shared a platter.

"It's sort of weird to have cold roast pork for breakfast," Scott said.

"All these people are eating as if they don't know when they'll get another meal," Chester pointed out. "Maybe we should, too." He picked up a bone and started to gnaw on it.

The lord of the castle stood up. "Good morning, gentlemen," he said. "If any of you wish to go to the fair in Mansfield, you may join the company that will leave the inner gate in an hour's time."

"That would be a good place for you minstrels to be," the page boy next to Chester said.

Everybody seemed excited at the idea of the fair. They rushed to finish the meal. The pages hurried to clear away the remains of the food and take it out to the poor people waiting in the courtyard. Then they raced out to join the people gathering at the gate.

Rachel saw that Lady Isabel was talking to her mother. The countess shook her head, but Lady Isabel went on talking. The countess turned to the earl and said something. He talked to his daughter and then to the friar. The friar spoke for quite a long time. At last, the earl smiled and nodded to his daughter. Rachel saw Lady Isabel clasp her hands as if to keep from clapping for joy.

"What about it, kids," Chester said. "Do you want to go to the fair?"

"It must be fun. Everybody seems to be going," Scott told him.

The children followed Chester out of the great hall to the courtyard. They had to go through the thick wall to where the drawbridge went across the moat. Already a group of people was standing there, but Rachel saw that there were only ten knights in the company. She guessed the others were staying behind to guard the castle.

The knights were on horseback and wore heavy armor. Behind each knight came a squire, who was also on horseback. Both the knights and the squires carried swords.

The company seemed to be waiting for someone. Finally, Lady Isabel came riding through the gate on a little white horse. Ethel rode behind her on a donkey.

All the knights and their squires raised their swords in greeting to the earl's daughter. A knight on a coal-black horse rode forward to lead Lady Isabel to her place in the cavalcade.

Five knights and their squires rode first across the bridge. Then came Lady Isabel and Ethel. After them walked Rachel,

Scott, and Chester, along with the page boys and many of the people from the courtyard. The other five knights and their squires rode in the rear.

They crossed the drawbridge and trooped through the gate in the outer wall of the castle to the bright green fields on the other side.

19

"Come and walk beside me, Rachel," Lady Isabel said. "I'm glad you also are going to the fair. We can get to know each other better."

Lady Isabel was wearing a long blue dress. She was riding with both her legs on the same side of the horse.

"Is the town far from here?" Rachel asked.

"I could get there in an hour if I were allowed to ride like a boy," the earl's daughter told her, "but I'm lucky my father let me go at all. The friar told him it was time I saw something of the world outside the castle. I've never been to the fair before."

"Scott and I went to a fair last summer. It was lots of fun," Rachel said. "We ate cotton candy and rode on the ferris wheel."

The narrow dirt road wound between green fields where people were working. They bowed and touched their foreheads as the company from the castle passed them. Rachel waved to a girl with a hooked stick who was guiding a flock of sheep across the road.

On the other side of the fields, the knights led the way into a dark wood. Great spreading trees hung over the road.

"There are outlaws in these woods," Lady Isabel said.

The horsemen rode faster, and the people on foot had to walk faster to keep up with them. Rachel couldn't talk to Lady Isabel now.

The forest seemed to go on and on. Rachel was getting tired. Scott started to lag behind. Chester took hold of Rachel's hand on one side and Scott's on the other. "We'd better keep together," he said. "I wouldn't want you kids getting lost here."

The sun was climbing higher in the sky. Here and there a shaft of light came through the leaves. Rachel wanted to stop and listen to the blackbird singing in an old oak tree and take a drink from the cool water of a spring that bubbled beside the road. But she had to keep walking.

At last they came out of the shadows of the forest. Up ahead, the roofs and spires of a town were shining in the sunlight.

"That is Mansfield," Lady Isabel said.

20

Rachel hoped the knights would go more slowly now that they were out of the woods. Instead, the sight of the town seemed to excite them. They rode even faster.

Everybody wanted to get to the market square, which was lined with stalls where things were for sale. When they reached the square, they rushed around, trying to see and do everything in the time before they would have to go back to the castle.

Rachel had a funny feeling that some of the women were staring at her. She stayed close to Chester and Scott.

The three of them walked past the booth where people were buying woolen cloth. They stopped to watch a tinker who was mending copper pots, and they looked at brass buttons and buckles that were for sale.

Scott stopped at a stand where a woman was selling caps. He picked up a brown leather cap with a blue feather on it. "Let's see if this fits you, Chester."

Chester tried it on. Both Rachel and Scott liked the way he looked in it so much that Chester bought the cap.

A huge cask of ale was set up under an awning. The knights were drinking big mugs of it.

Chester bought a basket of blackberries from a little girl. Rachel and Scott helped him eat them. They all drank water from the well in the marketplace. Then Chester took the children into a cookshop. They bought something the woman making them called "cakes." These seemed more like cookies to Scott and Rachel.

In the center of the square, the knights were looking at horses. Lady Isabel wanted to buy a speckled-gray pony, but the knight in charge of the company talked her out of it.

Chester took out his mouth organ and began to play "Home on the Range." This was one of Mr. Walker's favorites. Scott and Rachel knew the words. They sang it all the way through.

Even the knights joined in singing this

time, along with the pages, and all the people in the market square. Everybody held hands and danced around and around.

Chester played and played, and the people danced as if they'd never stop. Lady Isabel looked as if she'd never had so much fun in all her life.

Afterward Scott passed around the new cap, and the dancers filled it with silver coins.

21

The sun was still high in the sky when the squires rounded up the people from the castle for the return journey.

The knights were sleepy from the ale they had drunk. Everybody was worn out from dancing. They all went slower than in the morning.

Ethel rode beside Lady Isabel and talked to her as they jogged along.

After they came to the forest Lady Isabel's little horse began to limp. She stopped riding. The whole company came to a halt.

The knight in charge rode over to see what was wrong. "Your horse has lost a shoe. I'll send two of the squires back to look for it. In the meantime, we can all give our horses a rest." He got off his horse and helped the earl's daughter down from hers.

Lady Isabel sat on a mossy bank under an enormous beech tree. Ethel tied her donkey to a bush and came over to be near her.

Scott and Chester walked around looking at the horses and talking to the squires who tended them.

Lady Isabel patted the soft moss beside her. "Sit here, Rachel. I haven't seen much

of you all day. And there's something I must tell you."

Rachel sat down beside her. The earl's daughter spoke in a very low voice. "Ethel has been talking to her friends today. What the people from the castle are saying about you is frightening. And I'm afraid some of it is my fault."

"What do you mean?" Rachel asked.

"They say you are a witch and have put a spell on me." Lady Isabel's eyes filled with tears. "They saw us talking this morning by the well and again when you walked beside my horse." She looked around. "And my sitting by you now will make things even worse.

"Oh, Rachel, you can't know how wonderful it is for me to talk to you. I feel as if I could tell you all my thoughts. The friar is the only other person I can really talk to. But he's a man and can't understand the things that trouble me."

Rachel looked around. The knights and squires and the other men were busy talking to each other. But the women and girls were silently watching Rachel and Lady Isabel.

Rachel wanted to take her friend's hand, but she couldn't let the watching eyes see her do it. "Why do they think I'm a witch? I didn't turn you into a frog. And I didn't fly here on a broom."

Lady Isabel laughed. Then she was serious again. "It's not a joke, Rachel. The friar reads a great deal, and he is wiser than anyone else here. But even he can't explain how you got here or where you came from."

"I can't explain it, either," Rachel said. "It was magic all right, but it wasn't wicked magic. Not at all!"

"I believe you, Rachel," Lady Isabel said, "but no one else will. The most difficult thing for the women to understand is the way the man and boy who are your companions treat you. They are sure you have them in your power and have put them under a terrible spell."

22

Rachel stared at Lady Isabel. "I don't understand why anybody would think I had Scott and Chester in my power. Can you tell me?"

"It's because," Lady Isabel whispered, "they never give you orders!"

Rachel laughed. "But Scott's my little brother. And Chester isn't my father. He's just a friend. If he were my father, I'd have to obey him."

"My brother used to tell me what I could and could not do," Lady Isabel said.

"He's a page in my uncle's house now. If my father were not here, both my mother and I would have to do whatever my brother wanted."

Rachel thought about this. "You mean, even when you're grown up, your brother could boss you?"

"Unless I was married," Lady Isabel said. "Then my husband would give me orders."

"Couldn't you marry someone who wasn't the bossy sort?" Rachel asked.

"I'll have to marry the man my father chooses for me," Lady Isabel told her.

For a minute Rachel didn't say anything. Then she cried, "That's awful!"

Lady Isabel took both Rachel's hands in her own. She looked into her eyes. "It isn't nearly as awful as what people do to witches," she said. "Rachel, you have to get away. They're talking about putting you in chains and throwing you in the dungeon of the castle. That's a horrible place, damp and dark and full of rats." Lady Isabel made her voice very low. "*Terrible* things are done to witches, Rachel. It isn't safe for you to go back to the castle."

Rachel felt for the magic sizer in the pocket of her jeans. Then she began to search in all her other pockets. She couldn't find the sizer in any of them.

Rachel ran her fingers over the mossy bank, but the sizer was not there.

It might be back in the market square, she thought, or lying somewhere along the road where Rachel had walked today. There was no use looking for it, because the sizer was invisible until someone touched it.

Rachel felt sick. She was sure of only one thing—now neither she nor Scott could ever go home again.

23

The two squires came galloping down the dirt road. They had found the missing horseshoe near a patch of daisies.

With the help of the blacksmith, the squires nailed the shoe back on the horse's hoof. The cavalcade started off again.

When the knights rode out of the forest and along the road through the green fields, the sky was beginning to turn pink.

Rachel was walking between Scott and Chester. She had said nothing to them of Lady Isabel's warning. Maybe if she told Scott to order her around, the women would stop thinking she had enchanted him. But Rachel was afraid Scott would make a game of it. And she was sure she'd end up screaming at him.

There was no sense in frightening them. Anyway, if anything happened to her, Rachel somehow knew that Chester would take care of Scott.

Chester had put the coins they had earned into the purse the earl had given him. He wore the brown cap with the blue feather pushed back on his red hair and strode along with his head held high. "I never knew what I wanted to do for a living," he told the children. "I like being a minstrel better than anything I've ever done."

Scott was quiet. Then he said, "Maybe

you could get a job playing the mouth organ when we go home."

"Are you thinking of going home soon?" Chester asked.

"Well, I want to see Mom and Dad," Scott told him. "And these kids aren't much fun. All they talk about is fighting. That's just about the only thing anybody ever teaches them." Scott kicked a lump of dirt. "Besides, I'd like a bowl of cornflakes for breakfast and a chocolate chip ice cream cone once in a while."

Rachel listened in silence. Then she said, "Chester, if you had a chance, would you want to stay here?"

"Yes," he said. "I've heard that minstrels are welcome wherever they go. They bring the only news and music the people here have. I like ice cream just as much as Scott does, and I still remember the giant brownie you gave me for supper. But there are other things that matter more. I could be happy eating blackberries and playing my mouth organ."

"But what about your family? Won't they wonder what happened to you?" Scott asked.

"My mother and father were circus people," Chester told him. "They were killed in an accident when I was twelve. I grew up taking care of myself by doing odd jobs in circuses and carnivals. I've been traveling around, looking for a place to call home. Now, at last, I've found it."

In the distance, they could make out the tops of the square towers. They walked behind the knights and squires until they came to the outer wall of the castle. The men at arms inside opened the heavy gate, and the cavalcade rode through it onto the drawbridge.

It was nearly dark by the time Scott, Chester, and Rachel started over the bridge.

Rachel's heart was beating fast. Would there be people inside the castle waiting for her with chains?

Chester was talking. Rachel was glad to think about something else.

"Last night I had a hard time getting to sleep," he was saying. "I kept rolling onto something hard and lumpy on that tabletop."

"Like *The Princess and the Pea*," Scott said.

"Exactly," Chester agreed. "I finally got hold of the thing and stuffed it into my jacket pocket. Let's see if it's still there." He was carrying his jacket, and he had to unroll it to get at the pocket.

Rachel looked up to see the first star of evening shining in the sky. She made a wish.

Chester pulled something out of his pocket. "I'd like to give you a present, Rachel. I don't know what it's good for, except for you to remember me by." He handed her a little two-headed hammer of clear plastic.

Rachel ran her fingers over the magic sizer. "Thank you, Chester," she said. "I can use it." She touched his arm, "Chester, if you really want to stay here, go into the castle and leave us outside. And if we don't see you again, good luck!"

They had come to the other side of the bridge. Chester bent down and hugged them both at the same time. Then he walked through the open gate into the castle courtyard.

Rachel pulled Scott into the shadows. She waited until the last knight and squire had galloped over the bridge and through the gate. Then she went over to the castle wall and tapped it three times with the big hammerhead.

24

As soon as she touched it, the castle started to shrink.

Scott was standing next to Rachel. She had a tight grip on his arm.

In almost no time, he blinked and looked around. "Hey, Rachel, we're back in my room!"

Rachel let go of her brother's arm. "And there's the castle." She pointed to the floor.

The castle was once more the one they had made with the Build-Anything Kit. The big blue box was beside it.

Rachel was still holding the magic hammer. She bent down and put it into the box with the rest of the kit. Then she put the lid on the box.

There was the sound of the front door opening downstairs. Scott and Rachel heard their mother calling them. They ran

downstairs. Mr. and Mrs. Walker were in the front hall.

"Hi, kids!" Mr. Walker went to hang his coat in the hall closet.

Rachel picked up the package from the chair in the hall and gave it to her mother.

Mrs. Walker handed it to her husband. "What's this?" he asked.

"Something I saw an ad for," Mrs. Walker told him. "It seemed like something you would like."

Mr. Walker held up a booklet—"Instructions." There was another book in the package, too. Mr. Walker put both of them on the table and dug down into the box to pull out something wrapped in cotton.

"How did you know I've always wanted one of these? And this one is such a beauty!" He held up a shiny new mouth organ.

"This is a music book, Dad!" Scott said.

Rachel opened the book to the first page. "You can learn to play 'Home on the Range.'"